To Paul, Danette, Laura, & Erin

From Bret Nicholaus

Paul Lowrim

Enjoy the conversations!!

The

Mom & Dad

Conversation

Piece

By Bret Nicholaus and Paul Lowrie

The Conversation Piece
The Christmas Conversation Piece
The Mom & Dad Conversation Piece

The Mom & Dad Conversation Piece

Creative Questions to Celebrate the Family

**Bret Nicholaus
and Paul Lowrie**

Ballantine Books   New York

Library of Congress Catalog Card Number: 97-93275

ISBN: 345-40713-X

Manufactured in the United States of America

First Edition: May 1997

10   9   8   7   6   5   4   3   2   1

To my mom and late dad, for their unceasing support, immeasurable self-sacrifice, and limitless love!

To my wife and best friend, Christina, for saying "yes" to the most important question I've ever asked her.

—Bret Nicholaus

To my mom and dad for their unending love.

—Paul Lowrie

Mutual thanks:

To Joseph Purepos, literary agent, his wife, Betty, and our friend, Randy Bray, for their help on this project.

To our Lord Jesus Christ, who guides us daily through the greatest commandment: "Love the Lord your God with all your heart and with all your soul and with all your mind," and secondly, "Love your neighbor as yourself." (Mathew 22:37–40).

Welcome

...to moms, dads, sons, and daughters everywhere

Whether you own the title of mom or dad for yourself or have a mom or dad (or both) that you care about and love, you'll find this collection of questions to be a wonderful keepsake that can be enjoyed and cherished forever. While we all, predictably, know much about our own moms and dads, there are some things that we've never asked—

but would love to know. And there are many things that our parents would love to share—but have never told. This book gives moms and dads the opportunity to share favorite childhood memories, family values, vacation experiences, and words of wisdom they hope will be followed even after they're gone; it also encourages parents of all ages to share their most exciting moments in life, as well as the dreams and aspirations they still hold for the future.

In today's fast-paced world, the art of conversation—and certainly the sharing of ourselves with others—seems to have diminished. This book of questions allows conversation to take on a whole new meaning—one that appropriately benefits parents as well as children. Mom can share those important aspects of life that she wants to impart to her children; Dad can pass along the thoughts that he deems significant; and children (young or old) will be able to more fully appreciate who their parents are. Though many of the questions go well beyond typical triviality, you'll find that there is always an entertaining quality about the questions—and that even the most thought-provoking queries are *positive* in nature.

Because of the fun, entertaining style of the questions, moms or dads buying this book for family use will find that even young children will be interested in the answers, not to mention the questions themselves. If you are an adult giving this book to your mom or dad, you know how valuable their thoughts and experiences in life can be and will find that these questions will enrich your conversations with them.

Keep in mind that this book can be enjoyed with friends as easily as with family members, since it provides as many good laughs as it does opportunities for serious contemplation. Then again, you may decide simply to read the questions to yourself as you reflect on your life and that of your children. (Just because the word *conversation* appears in the title doesn't mean this book can't be experienced equally well in the silence of your own bedroom!) *We do encourage moms and dads to consider writing down their answers; this will provide a priceless keepsake for your children.* However you decide to enjoy the book, make sure you do just that—enjoy it! And may we find as sons and daughters—or as moms and dads—that parents truly are treasure chests of insights, memories, and inspiration; we need only give them the chance to open up to us!

"The important thing is the family. If you can keep the family together . . . that's what we hope to do."

—WALT DISNEY

The

Mom & Dad

Conversation

Piece

1

For each of your children, where were you and what were you doing when you realized that it was definitely time for your baby to be born?

2

When you were growing up, what was dinnertime like in your home? What was a typical meal?

3

What are some of the very first things you can remember teaching your children to do?

4

When did your dad or mom first let you get behind the wheel of the car? What was your most interesting experience when you were learning to drive?

5

Who is the most famous person you've ever met face-to-face?

6

What is something you and your spouse have always done together that many couples would consider trite and boring, but that the two of you find very meaningful?

7

Who was your best friend in high school? What made you and your friend so compatible?

8

What is the greatest lesson your children have ever taught you?

9

As a child, what was your favorite family tradition?

10

As a parent, what family tradition is or was the most meaningful for you?

11

What was your first car? What one feature above all others made it special to you?

12

If you could go back to the beginning and start over, what particular job or career do you think you would've really enjoyed pursuing?

13

What trip above all others do you think is best enjoyed when taken by car?

14

If a tree were going to be planted in your honor—or, ultimately, in your memory—what type of tree would you want it to be?

15

Virtually everyone remembers what he or she was doing when the news came. Where were you and what were you doing when you learned of the John F. Kennedy assassination?

16

When you were growing up, what was the most memorable family vacation you ever took?

17

As a mom or dad yourself, what has been the most memorable vacation you and your children have taken?

18

If you could pass down one—and only one—family recipe to your children, which recipe would you choose?

19

We're used to describing ourselves in terms of height, hair color, and eye color; but how would you describe your *smile* to someone? Be as detailed as you can.

20

Whose party (birthday, anniversary, retirement, and the like) above all others will you never forget?

21

What is one childlike quality that you have maintained throughout your life?

22

With respect to raising your children, what is your greatest accomplishment?

23

Who is one friend from yesteryear whom you've completely lost contact with, but with whom you would love to somehow reestablish ties?

24

What is your favorite wedding-day memory?

25

What daily time or activity do you treasure more than any other?

26

Clothing trends and styles come and go, but each of us has a favorite. What has been your favorite clothing trend/style over the years?

27

Why did you choose the names that you did for your children? How easy was it to decide on the names?

28

What particular childhood Christmas memory do you remember most fondly?

29

What particular Christmas memory as a parent do you treasure the most?

30

If you could choose only one famous quote that you would want your children to always remember, which one would it be?

31

What was your favorite record to listen to growing up?

32

What TV mom or dad do you think you are most similar to?

33

When you were growing up, what did you get into trouble for more often than anything else?

34

Which of your birthdays did you anticipate with the greatest joy?

35

Each of us can probably name an age we *didn't* want to turn. What birthday were you the least enthusiastic to celebrate at the time?

36

What is the most daring feat you've ever accomplished (or tried to accomplish) during your lifetime?

37

If you were asked to choose the "family movie of the decade," what film would get your top vote?

38

What is one family vacation you have never taken but would still love to take someday?

39

What specific thing was the most enjoyable for you to teach your children?

40

If money were not a concern, what do you believe would be the ideal number of children to have?

41

Virtually everyone can recall a household accident like falling off a ladder. What is your most interesting mishap at home?

42

If you were allowed to keep only one family photograph, which one would you choose? How old are the children in this picture?

43

If you could add one room onto the house that would serve any unique purpose you desired, what would the room be?

44

In your opinion, what quality above all others is essential to instill in children today?

45

We're all experts at something (if only in our own minds). What particular topic do you believe you know well enough that you could at least entertain the thought of writing a book about it?

46

What is your favorite song of all time?

47

What was the most exciting sports moment you ever witnessed?

48

What has been the best five-year period of your life thus far?

49

W hat toy from your childhood did you
treasure above all others?

50

B esides a spouse or a child, what has been
the greatest blessing in your life?

51

What one article of clothing (besides a wedding dress) will you probably always hold on to because of its sentimental value?

52

What activity or event above all others do you think every family should experience together at least once?

53

Besides a family member, which person (living or deceased) has had the greatest influence on your becoming the person you are today?

54

Besides a family member, is there any person whose life you feel you've in some way made better?

55

What is the greatest book you've ever read?

56

In your opinion, what would be the ideal place (city, state, geographic location, and the like) in which to raise a family?

57

What is the best clean joke you've ever heard?

58

If you could have a one-hour conversation with any person in your family's history, whom would you choose? What specific questions would you ask of him or her?

59

If you had the chance to take another honeymoon, where would you most want to go?

60

What was the most unusual hairstyle you ever had?

61

In general, at what age do you think children are the cutest to observe?

62

In the classroom of life, what lesson do you believe we must continuously try to master day after day?

63

If you had to pick one particular aspect that makes a house a home, what would it be?

64

As a child, what was the first "business" venture you ever undertook? (Example: A lemonade stand.)

65

If you had more time on your hands, what hobby would you most like to pursue diligently?

66

What is the oldest keepsake in your possession?

67

In your opinion, what is the secret of life?

68

What is the greatest goal you want to achieve within the next five years?

69

What has been your greatest personal accomplishment in life?

70

What faraway friends whom you seldom get to see anymore do you wish you could visit more frequently?

71

Who was your favorite actor or actress when you were a teenager? Who is your all-time favorite actor or actress?

72

With respect to your spouse, when or how did you know that you were truly in love?

73

What were the very first fully understandable words that your baby spoke?

74

You should never measure a person's success by the size of his or her wallet. How do *you* measure a person's success in life?

75

What particular Father's Day and/or Mother's Day do you remember the most?

76

Besides the actual birth of your children, what has been your proudest moment as a mom or dad?

*S*omeday, when the pressures of raising a family are well behind you, you may actually find time to start writing the Great American Novel. As the author, what would you choose for the setting and the plot?

78

What is the most important thing that your parents did in raising you that you also did—or are doing—in raising *your* children?

79

What is the oldest photograph you have of someone in your family's history?

80

If you had the power to solve one—and only one—problem in the world today, what problem would you eradicate?

81

Suppose that you were asked to make a 15-minute videotape of yourself that would give your children something to remember you by when you're deceased. Assuming that this will be the only video of you available to your children, what would you want to be doing on the tape?

82

What was the weather like on the day you got married?

83

Suppose you could combine the personalities and attributes of any three people in history to create the consummate mom or dad. Which three people would you choose?

84

What is the best birthday gift you can remember receiving?

85

For today's teens, the local mall seems to be the popular spot to rendezvous. Where was your favorite spot to "hang out" when you were a teenager?

86

As a mom, what do you think is the most difficult aspect of being a dad in today's world?

87

As a dad, what do you think is the most difficult aspect of being a mom in today's world?

88

Besides something directly related to the family (i.e., the birth of a child), what has been the most exciting day of your life?

89

Many people carry something they treasure in their wallet. Besides a picture of family members, is there any really meaningful item that you keep with you in your wallet?

90

Where did you get engaged? How was the marriage proposal made?

91

What one Scripture verse or other powerful instruction for living do you hope your children will always remember?

92

What was one negative in your life that you were somehow able to turn into something quite positive?

93

If you were writing your memoirs today, what would be the most appropriate title?

94

Besides hugs and kisses, what do you believe is the best way to show your children that you really love them?

95

If you were making a list of your three favorite childhood memories, what would the entries be?

96

What is something that most parents would consider a chore that you actually enjoy (or have enjoyed) doing?

97

What is the kindest thing a stranger has ever done for you?

98

In your opinion, what has been the biggest news event (national or international) during your lifetime?

99

What was your favorite household scent as a child?

100

Over the course of your life, what would you say has been your favorite room in the house?

101

What were your parents' most distinguishing physical features?

102

What is something memorable that you once saw or did that your children will probably never have the opportunity to see or experience? (Example: Talking to a veteran of World War I.)

103

Dads (or moms): What is your favorite food to throw on the grill?

104

Moms (or dads): What is your favorite item to bake?

105

If you could relive one full year of your life exactly as it originally happened, to what year would you return?

106

Suppose that a movie were going to be made about your life. Who do you think would be best suited to play you in the film?

107

If you had to describe your disposition in terms of a musical instrument, which one would you choose?

108

Is there anyone you know of in your family's history who had an encounter with or knew someone famous?

109

What was your favorite grade in school?

110

What do you remember most about your first Christmas as a mom or dad?

111

Most moms and dads have at one time or another taken something away from a child as an appropriate form of punishment. If a child were going to similarly punish you as an adult for doing something wrong, what would you find most difficult to give up?

112

Thanksgiving and Christmas seem to get all the credit when it comes to memorable holidays. So . . . what was a typical Fourth of July celebration like for you when you were a child?

113

Suppose that you were asked to sketch out on paper your family tree. What type of tree would represent your family? Be creative!

114

When you have bad days, what is the best thing you can do to make yourself happy again?

115

If you could pass along only one piece of advice on how to feel fulfillment in life, what would you say?

116

What are your three all-time greatest memories as a parent?

117

What is the silliest, most off-the-wall thing you've ever done in your life?

118

What word or short phrase do you think more people need to say more often?

119

As a young child, what was your favorite children's book to read?

120

What has been the most enjoyable club, league, or team to which you have ever belonged?

121

What is something you've always wished you could do well, but as yet have not been able to master?

122

Kids do say the darnedest things! What is something your child once said at a young age that you'll never forget?

123

Besides eating right and exercising, what do you believe is the key to living a healthy life?

124

What one topic above all others do you believe a person should avoid discussing with other people?

125

Everyone has a purpose for being here. What have you come to see as your place in this world?

126

What is the best piece of advice you've ever received?

127

What is the best piece of advice you've ever given to your children?

128

Excluding any family members, which particular person whom you know do you have the most respect for?

129

If you had to pick one thing that every boy should have while growing up, what would it be?

130

If you had to pick one thing that every girl should have while growing up, what would it be?

131

If you were attending a large party where you didn't know any of the guests, what type of person (in terms of personality, lifestyle, etc.) would you be most prone to seek out?

132

What is the best class you've ever taken in your life?

133

In terms of mannerisms or physical appearance, have you ever been compared to a famous person? If so, whom?

134

Which of life's mysteries are you most curious about?

135

What is the highest honor or award you've ever received in your life?

136

In your opinion, what is the ideal age to become a parent?

137

What is the most memorable family outing you've ever taken with your children?

138

Just for fun, have you ever added up how much money you've earned to this point in your life?

139

What is the very first thing that you can clearly remember from your childhood?

140

Suppose that all the cards from a standard deck were lying faceup in front of you on a table. If you had to pick 1 of the 52 cards to abstractly represent your life, which card would you choose?

141

In terms of numbers, what is the largest Thanksgiving Day celebration you've ever been a part of?

142

What is your most memorable
Thanksgiving Day experience?

143

Which particular attribute of your own
mom do you see the most in yourself?

144

Which particular attribute of your own
dad do you see the most in yourself?

145

W hat would you list as the three most memorable TV moments you've ever seen?

146

W hat professional athlete or otherwise famous person do you believe is the best role model for children today?

147

W hat famous person (living or deceased) do you think every adult would do well to try and emulate?

148

What were the big events going on in the world the year you were born? Who was president?

149

What would you choose as the greatest accomplishment or development in the world during your lifetime?

150

When you meet people for the first time, what are you generally the most interested in learning about them?

151

What was your first full-time job? Do you remember what your hourly pay was?

152

What is the most valuable fact or insight that you have learned during the past year?

153

What is the most memorable road you've ever driven on?

154

Over the course of your life, what activity has most consistently given you a feeling of inner peace?

155

As a child, who was your hero (fictitious or real)?

156

If you had more time in the day, what would you spend it doing?

157

As far as you know, who in your family's history has lived the longest?

158

Besides, quite obviously, being in love, what do you think is the key to a successful marriage?

159

As a youngster, whose house did you always look forward to visiting?

160

If you had to give yourself an appropriate sobriquet (Abraham Lincoln's was "Honest Abe"), what would it be?

161

During your life, have you ever celebrated your birthday the same day that a major news event was occurring?

162

Suppose that three objects that you own were going to be buried in a time capsule to be opened by future family members 100 years from now. What three objects would give them the most valuable insight as to who you were as a person?

163

If you could leave your loved ones only three instructions to get them through life successfully, which three would you choose?

164

In your opinion, what is the greatest comfort of home—tangible or intangible?

165

Do you generally live your life for the present or for the future?

166

What one thing above all others did you really dislike as a child that you have come to fully appreciate as an adult?

167

Allowing for exceptions to the rule, what is something you truly believe dads will always be better at than moms when it comes to raising kids?

168

Allowing for exceptions to the rule, what is something you truly believe moms will always be better at than dads when it comes to raising kids?

169

In your opinion, what has been the biggest change in the way people think or act since your childhood?

170

What is the longest project you've ever worked on?

171

Where have the best times of your life taken place?

172

With what famous person's life story do you think every adult should be familiar?

173

If you had to make a "Top Ten" list of people you've met over the years who represent the best that humankind has to offer, who would make this elite list?

174

What's the best gift you ever received from your children?

175

What is the most interesting thing that happened on your honeymoon?

176

What event/occurrence in your past changed your life for the better more than any other?

177

As a mom or dad with older children, what is your favorite thing to do with your son or daughter?

178

As a mom or dad with younger children, what was—or is—your favorite activity to do with your son or daughter?

179

What was the most mischievous thing you can recall doing as a young child?

180

If you had had another baby girl, what would you have been likely to name her?

181

If you had had another baby boy, what might you have chosen as his name?

182

Suppose that each family in the neighborhood had to put a Christmas ornament on the town tree. Assuming that the ornament was supposed to represent your family's ideals, what would it look like?

183

As a parent, what were your thoughts the first day your child went off to kindergarten?

184

Do you have any recollections of your *own* days in kindergarten?

185

When you were a very young child, what did you want to be when you grew up? When you were in high school, what did you think you would be doing for a living someday?

186

What is one family tradition that you have not yet experienced but would love to start?

187

When you think of your hometown, what image pops into your mind first?

188

In children's bedrooms today—especially teenagers' rooms—one is likely to find posters or pictures tacked to the walls. What did your bedroom walls, dressers, and the like display as a teenager?

189

Did your mom and dad have favorite expressions they would always say? If so, what were they?

190

What fad can you remember *really* getting into as a child? Any favorite fads as an adult?

191

Every family has at least one element that makes it truly unique. What was one of the more unique aspects of your family when you were growing up?

192

What is one of the unique aspects of your own family today?

193

Assume for a moment that you could actually decide exactly how you want to look (i.e., physical characteristics). In an ideal world, how would you look? Be as specific as you can.

194

When you turn your thoughts to your children, what makes you the most proud?

195

As a child, what was your favorite pet?

196

Almost all of us wish our lives could be more relaxing and simplified. If you could use only three key words, how would you best describe "the simple life" as you wish it could be?

197

What was the first "big" item that you bought after you were married?

198

What is one buzzword or phrase that was highly popular during your teenage years?

199

What was your favorite game to play as a child? What's your all-time favorite game as an adult?

200

Regardless of what was going on in your personal life, what year during your lifetime would you have liked to have been stuck in, yourself aging at a normal rate, but with society basically staying the same forever after?

201

How many different states have your ancestors lived in?

202

What is the earliest lesson you can remember learning as a child that you have followed throughout your life?

203

If you could've been born in any year before or after the year you were *actually* born, what year would you choose?

204

In your opinion, what would have been the ideal time of year (month and date) for you to have been born?

205

How old were you when you went on your very first date? Where did you go?

206

Did you ever have a special hiding place as a child?

207

What was your favorite summertime activity when you were growing up?

208

Approximately how many students were in your high school graduating class?

209

If 20 people who know you were asked to describe you using only one adjective, what do you think would be the most popular word used?

210

When did your children take their first baby steps?

211

What is the most memorable phone call you've ever received?

212

Walt Disney, no stranger to tough times, once said, "I think it's important to have a good hard failure when you're young." Do you agree or disagree with his statement? Why?

213

What is the greatest distance you've ever traveled by car for a family vacation?

214

When you think of all the photographs you've taken on your family vacations, which one comes to mind first?

215

As a child, what did you wish for more often and/or more sincerely than anything else?

216

Mom: Besides physical appearance, which of Dad's qualities/personality traits initially attracted you to him?

217

Dad: Besides physical appearance, which of Mom's qualities/personality traits initially attracted you to her?

218

Can you recall a particular brand name that was extremely trendy during your teenage years?

219

Many young people today hear about the past and can't imagine life without some of today's conveniences. What is one modern-day convenience that you didn't have when growing up that, quite honestly, was easy to live without?

220

What is something you were initially reluctant to let your children have or do, but to which you ultimately acquiesced after much pleading and begging on their part?

221

What is the most memorable walk you've ever taken?

222

What is the most important text (or portion of text) you've ever memorized during your life?

223

When you look back on the life you've lived to this point, what amazes you the most?

224

What is one item you got rid of years ago that you wish you could have back?

225

When you were 16 years old, what do you remember being able to buy for one dollar?

226

What is the greatest leap of faith you've ever taken?

227

What was the most exciting event or occurrence that ever took place in your hometown?

228

Moms: What is something you truly appreciate or enjoy doing that most women probably don't care for?

229

D ads: What is something you truly
appreciate or enjoy doing that most
men probably don't care for?

230

I n your opinion, what is the highest
compliment anyone can receive?

231

Between fixing the home and fixing dinner, moms' and dads' hands are often full—literally! Over the years, with which tool, implement, or utensil have you felt the most at ease?

232

Over the course of your life, what have you probably spent more time pondering than anything else?

233

Suppose that upon your death a memorial fund were established in your name and that a substantial amount of money was received. For what purpose or cause would you want the money to be used?

234

Even though you probably weren't of any *real* assistance, with which household job did you love to help your mom or dad when you were a child?

235

What is the most romantic thing your spouse has ever done for you?

236

What was the address of your very first residence (i.e., your parents' address when you were born)?

237

Above everything else, what one thing do you personally believe all people should do or experience at least once in their lifetime—just to say they've done it?

238

What is your most interesting family-reunion memory?

239

During your first year or two of marriage, what illusion did you have about married life that you soon came to realize wasn't true?

240

"Knock on wood." Which aspect of your life thus far has luck generally seemed to favor?

241

Besides your own mom or dad, which family member (grandma, grandpa, aunt, uncle, etc.) do you think you physically resemble the most?

242

In what ways do you believe life is analogous to each of the following geographical features: a mountain, a river, and an open plain? Be creative, yet honest.

243

Before any of your children were actually born, how many children did you envision yourself having and what sex did you want them to be?

244

If you had to choose one thing you own that has more sentimental value than any other, what object would you pick?

245

If you could have a professional photograph taken of your family anywhere in the world (presumably somewhere from which a family photo doesn't already exist), where would you want the picture taken?

246

Of all the American presidents during your lifetime, which one has been your favorite?

247

What is the greatest compliment you've ever been paid?

248

If your life were literally flashing before your eyes, what are five moments or scenes that you would expect to stand out?

249

What one place above all others do you like to go to when you need peace, quiet, and time for reflection?

250

At some point in your life, you no doubt knew someone who did something for you, seemingly insignificant at the time, that ultimately had a profound impact on the direction your life took (personally or professionally). Who was it, what did he or she do, and how has it affected your life?

251

In terms of the big picture, what surprises you most about life? (Example: Its brevity.)

252

Looking back to when you were 21 years old, what was your biggest misconception about how your own future would unfold?

253

Moms: If you could receive a bouquet consisting of three different kinds of flowers, which three would you want in the arrangement?

254

Dads: What is (or was) your favorite tie? Did you ever wear a tie you didn't like simply because your child gave it to you as a gift?

255

Did you ever do anything for your children that you *never* would have done for anyone else?

256

If you could choose only one question and corresponding answer from this book for your children to always remember, which one would it be?

A Note to Our Readers

Many of you have shared with us the creative ways you've found to use our books: in school classrooms; at dinner parties; in college dormitories; at family gatherings; at reunions; and during coffee breaks with friends or coworkers. We've even heard from folks who have found the books especially fun and entertaining on long car trips and when traveling by plane.

Please let us know how *you* are enjoying the books; we would love to hear from you. Write to us at the address below, and thank you for including us in your conversations!

Bret Nicholaus & Paul Lowrie
P.O. Box 340
Yankton, SD 57078

About the Authors

Bret Nicholaus and **Paul Lowrie** are 1991 graduates of Bethel College, St. Paul, Minnesota. They hold their degrees in public relations/advertising and marketing, respectively. Both authors are firmly committed to providing positive entertainment for adults and children alike. "We share many of the same visions and values that Walt Disney had," says Lowrie. Nicholaus adds, "We want to give people the chance to dream of a world where possibilities are endless, while encouraging a sincere appreciation for the past." They have collaborated on two previous popular books, *The Conversation Piece* and *The Christmas Conversation Piece*.